Simplify And Organize By 5 O'clock!

Organize

Organize Your Mind And Life With Fast And Simple Techniques For Decluttering And Organizing, Increasing Concentration, Motivation, And Productivity!

Ryan Cooper

STOP!!! Before you read any further....Would you like to know the secrets of Anti-Aging?

If your answer is yes, then you are not alone. Thousands of people are looking for the secret to reducing wrinkles, looking younger, and maintaining a youthful appearance.

If you have been searching for these answers without much luck, you are in the right place!

Not only will you gain incredible insight in this book, but because I want to make sure to give you as much value as possible, right now for a limited time you can get full **100% FREE access to a VIP bonus EBook** entitled **Anti-Aging Made Easy!**

Just Go Here For Free Instant Access:

www.LuxyLifeNaturals.com

Legal Notice

Disclaimer Notice

Table Of Contents

Introduction

I want to thank you and congratulate you for purchasing the book, *Organize: Simplify And Organize by 5 O'clock! - Organize Your Mind And Life With Fast And Simple Techniques For Decluttering And Organizing, Increasing Concentration, Motivation, And Productivity!"*.

This book contains proven steps and strategies on how to get rid of junk from your household and workplace so you can finally enjoy and make the most out of your life.

This book contains information that would help you gain an understanding on why clutter accumulates in your life. You would also find out about mistakes to keep an eye out for. This book will not only help you get rid of physical clutter – it would also help you clear your mind and be more organized in various aspects of your life. You would be introduced to the merits of a minimalist lifestyle, and how to adopt it.

Thanks again for purchasing this book, I hope you enjoy it!

Chapter 1: Top 10 Pitfalls Of Organization And Why We Let Our Lives Get Cluttered

A clean home is a comfortable and happy place. After all, coming home to a chaotic house invites confusion and even depression in its wake. On the other hand, being welcomed by tidy surroundings can help you relax more. Studies showed that this can help you have increased levels of productivity for other areas in your life.

Even with these benefits, a lot of people still have a hard time in maintaining a clutter-free life. In this chapter, we will discuss why it can be hard to let go of clutter, and why we seem to easily allow them to accumulate. We will also cover the more common pitfalls of organizing and how you can counteract them.

Why people allow so much clutter into their lives

A lot of people just seem to have a hard time letting go.

This is especially applicable to those who frequently move from one place to another. Some people feel good about stocking up on memorabilia. However, this will eventually hold you down in the long run because you have too much of the things that you really do not need in life.

Studies show that people feel the need for abundance most of the time.

This is especially true for people who have had a tough time making it through recession periods. You may not want to throw away your things because you fear that you will be less financially secured because of this.

There is often the mentality of keeping something just in case you need to use it in the future.

Although being prepared is useful, you also have to be realistic about it. In some cases, items get kept in storage for around a decade. If you weren't able to make use of a piece of clothing in 10 years, you probably aren't going to need it anytime soon.

You have that sense of obligation.

A lot of greeting cards and other gifts from loved ones tend to pile up because you think you need to keep them as a form of obligation from your relatives. Sometimes, you need to throw away or donate some of them if they take up too much space already.

There is a fear of 'losing' an important piece of memory once you get rid of an item.

You should also keep in mind that those are just physical objects. No matter what you do, memories will be more important than these things.

The 10 common pitfalls in organizing

1. *Organizing will make you spend a lot of time especially if you consider a lot of things as sentimental.*

   Organizing helps you create space for more important things and discard those that are not vital in your life. This is more on how you can get the most out of what you have in life at the moment. This is not only about obsessively arranging what you see on a regular basis but also about arranging the seemingly minor things.

2. *On organizing your things, you may commit the mistake of throwing away things that other members of your family may still need.*

    To help prevent this problem from taking shape, you should establish good communication lines with the people in your household. As much as possible, you have to encourage them to join you in organizing everything so nothing useful will be thrown away.

3. *If you make major organizing system changes in an instance, you may be required to spend a lot of money.*

    Therefore, the best way to go is to spend on organizing tools little by little. Because you do not have thoughtless last-minute purchases, you can eventually save up the money or buy other things that you plan to.

4. *Being indecisive on which system to use on a long-term basis may ruin the initial goal of organizing for you.*

    Using even just a single system that works wonderfully for you will help you achieve a greater sense of balance for your life. In turn, this can help you take care of your health and your family even more.

5. *If you are a person who easily panics at the prospect of a relatively large task, organizing may bring you some level of stress especially at the onset of the activity.*

    To help deal with this concern, you have to initially agree on a given set of organizing system and be consistent with this. This will not only bring less stress for your family but also more uniformity.

6. *Focusing only on a single small area of the household or workplace that you have to organize may hamper your potential to improve the system for your home and workplace.*

   This happens if you get overwhelmed with what you have to organize. A good way to go around this problem is to gradually expand the areas where you will arrange your items. Doing this will help you organize everything before you know it.

7. *Holding on to things and forgetting to assess their absolute value in the long run will make you end up with a lot of items that you have to organize without much success.*

   This will eventually bring you a lot of stress. On top of that, this can make you end up feeling unmotivated and tired. Because you have to deal with a lot of "sentimental items", the clutter can get in the way of your daily activities. Getting rid of these things can help you fully experience a sense of freedom.

8. *Overworking your way to organize everything in a day is one of the most common pitfalls.*

   Studies show that those who organize their things and their tasks well perceive a full sense of energy within them. Just remember not to overdo it or your health and your quality time with other people might suffer.

9. *Spending unreasonable amounts of time in formulating goals will eat up large chunks of time that you can use to start off with organizing instead.*

   If you overdo planning, this may backfire. The best way to go around this pitfall is to make sure that you will allot a certain amount of time for this activity. You may spend one to two hours a week doing this.

10. *If you have not properly established what organizing system to use, you will end up making a bad example for your children.*

    If you are a homemaker, your children will usually learn from your organizing habits just from watching you do them. Showing them how they can be organized people will serve as a great lesson that they can always take for the remainder of their lives.

At first, it may seem almost impossible and difficult to organize your things and your entire. But as you go along, you will soon realize that doing so will help you enjoy other things in life. Understanding why you cannot seem to let go of some things easily will help you start off with organizing. Never again will you be entirely stuck in unwarranted overtimes and piles of unwanted garbage that needs to be thrown away a long time ago.

Chapter 2: Step 1 (Hour 1) - Organizing The Mind - If The Mind Is Organized The Rest Of Your Life Will Also Be Organized

Organizing is not just about tidying up items in your household and workplace. This also means that you have to set your activities and your state of mind in order. In this chapter, you will learn more on how you can improve your motivation and your concentration. If you can improve your current motivation levels, there is a great chance that you will strive harder to get what you want.

Before you start off identifying what you really want to achieve in life, you have to start off with a clean slate first.

You can do this by decluttering your mind. If you successfully do this, you will eventually end up finding your focus in life once more. Also, you will experience less stress. You can start by writing in a journal. This especially works well for your to-do tasks. If writing does not work for you, record them in your phone or any other device and retrieve the files later. You can also paint a picture, sketch a drawing, doodle – anything that would let you release whatever pent-up thoughts.

Determine where your priorities lie and the set goals.

As much as possible, you have to be specific about this. If you can break down your goal in smaller steps, this can make it even more specific. For a goal to be specific, you have to exactly state what you really want to accomplish in the long run. Filling out concerns like "who, what, when, where, why, and how" can help you do this.

In relation to this, make sure that the goal is measurable. This means that you have to know exactly how you will evaluate and observe if the goal has already been met. Specific values and parameters are some aspects that can help you measure your goals objectively.

You need to make sure that your goal is achievable as well. If you challenge and stretch your abilities to reach your goal, can you achieve this? Is this within reasonable level of difficulty? To make a set of goals achievable for you, you should not assign too many goals that you have to observe within a short period of time. Even if all of these are within reasonable range, it will be impossible to accomplish all of them at the same time.

If you broke down your goals into smaller ones, the smaller ones should be relevant to the larger goal. Also, these goals should go well with your key responsibilities to get what you want.

Finally, your goals should be time-bound. This means that you have to set a specific date or time when you should realize your goal. Set at least one target date. For more accurate assessment of completion, you may include frequency and deadlines to your goals.

Set all of your priorities straight.

- After knowing what you really want to achieve, you have to take a little break and rank your goals according to their importance to you.

- Take your routine into consideration. The way you currently live your life will tell you if you will get to your goals after some time. If there is a part of your lifestyle that does not sync well with these goals, you may have to modify or get rid of these altogether.

- Manage "urgent" tasks by completing them, getting rid of them, or delegating them. If something does not seem really important at the moment, you may opt to attend to that task after you have dealt with the more important ones.

In getting rid of clutter and knowing what you really want in life, you have to make sure that you will never bite off more than you can chew. Doing so will just contribute to more clutter in your life before you even know it. If you are going on a relatively slow phase in following the tips in this book section, fret not. As long as you are making some changes in your life, you are bound to end up with something big that will help you be successful in life.

Chapter 3: Step 2 (Hour 2) - The Purge And Declutter Movement - Get Rid Of All Distracting Ideals And Items

Distractions can significantly impair the productivity not just of a single person but also of a larger institution. This can even affect the quality of life of the person who has these distractions. In this book section, you will learn more about the concept of distracting ideals and items and how to deal with them.

There are two main types of distractions.

These are the good and the bad distracting items and ideals. Good distraction allows you to give way to opportunities for new rewards. Because rewards tend to provide you with that familiar feel-good sensation, this can help you tolerate stress and pain more effectively. On the other hand, bad distractions are those that you have not regulated well. They tend to eat up a lot of your time. Aside from having lower levels of productivity, this will make you end up accomplishing nothing in your life. In the long run, this may even lead to less satisfaction in life.

Identify and acknowledge distractions.

There are some common internal attitudes that can lead to more distractions in your life. Experts have pointed out at least three of them.

- Perfectionism made it to the top of their list. This applies for both your personal or professional project.

- People's inability to compromise can sometimes get in the way.

- If you are hesitant to ask for help from other people, chances are you are creating lots of distracting ideals for yourself.

How to clear your life of distracting ideals and items

You may start off with some items in your household that you have not got around to cleaning off. Starting off with your current mindset seems to work well for others, on the other hand. You may start off with either, as long as you get something done for a change. Consider the following:

If you have a set plan and someone suggests an easier way to accomplish things, maybe you want to reconsider that.

Failing to compromise may set up a barrier between your main goal and the people who can help you get to your goal in a faster and better way. In the process, you can even alienate those who are willing to help you finish off your tasks.

Placing a bulletin board to help hold notes regarding schedules, meetings, and other undertakings can help prevent the loss of important notes.

This will help you prevent writing things down on small scraps of paper that you may eventually lose. In the process, you will get rid of the stressful habit of hunting for these small papers. This simple act alone can then help eliminate a lot of distractions from your life.

Also, you may place a notepad and a pen next to your phone. You can use this to efficiently take down important bits of information from phone calls. Once you noted things down, you may decide to transfer this to your phonebook or simply post it on the bulletin board so the recipient will see.

If you are not used to ask for help, start off by creating the mindset that asking for some assistance is not a form of weakness in your part.

For large chunks of work, you may consider delegating smaller tasks to other people. You may even be surprised at their willingness to offer you their helping hands. At the end of the day, after they helped you out, do not forget to thank them. This will help make them feel useful and appreciated. Because of this, they may even be willing to help you the next time you ask for help again.

If you tend to be a perfectionist, keep in mind that flawless execution is not always important.

If you dwell too much time in changing small amounts of details in your work over and over, you will end up getting exhausted in the process. Because of this, you may find it difficult to proceed with the other tasks that you have at hand.

Make sure to set a specific date for reorganization.

Filing systems are not for all types of people. Even if they are, these systems have to be maintained no matter what. At least once a week or twice a month, set aside a specific day when you are required to go through most of your paper to sort them out. This will help keep things organized and clean for the long haul. Place this on your planner or calendar as a type of regular appointment. This will serve as a regular reminder that you have to do this task.

Chapter 4: Step 3 (Hour 3) - Embracing And Understanding The Minimalist Lifestyle

Cutting out on unnecessary things in your life can help make a large difference not just in your routine but in your overall health and viewpoint in life. In this book section, you will learn more about the concept of minimalism and what it can do for you in the long run.

Here are some benefits of a minimalist lifestyle

- You will end up having more financial freedom by spending less on things that you do not really need in the first place.

- If your home has minimalist design, you will end up experiencing less stress in the process.

- Because you can manage your home or office more readily, it will be easier for you to make them visually appealing.

- It would be easier for you to manage your home and your workplace.

- This is good for the environment because you will consume less substance that can readily harm your surroundings.

- You will be more productive because you have more free time in your hands.

- You can readily support some causes that you believe in.

- You will spend less time working for someone else.

- Working on things that you love will be one of your primary concerns.

- There will be fewer comparisons with other people.

- You can have more time for things that you deem important to you.

- You will not be tied to your past life anymore.

- Minimalism can help you invest and grow to pursue greater and more meaningful things in life.

- You can have more time for rest and relaxation.

You can perform various methods to help declutter for a more minimalist approach in life.

- Learn the basic mindset: only get and keep things that you actually need in your life.

- If you are to keep sentimental items, keep the most important ones that will not get in the way.

- Sort items according to an established system. For instance, you may sort your clothes according to the type of outfit and their colors, spice according to the kinds of dishes they would be good with. Make sure that you can maintain this system for long periods without spending too much time and effort.

- If you think you cannot get rid of everything at once, take everything slowly.

- Start throwing off things that you know you definitely will not be looking for in the future.

- Sell or donate things you do not need. It is easy enough to do this these days, thanks to craigslist and ebay.

- Hang coats using as little space as possible. You may hang them towards the end part of your closet rod. After this, you may freely use the area under them to store little items.

- Always ask yourself if you need a certain item when you shop for some items.

- Always keep your things in order. At this point, it is much easier because you have little to arrange.

- If you are just renting, consider moving out to a smaller living space.

Those who have already switched to a minimalist lifestyle have stated how much they are in tune with their life. Also, this has helped them make the most out of each day in their lives without having it too hard on themselves. Overall, they experience less stress in life while getting to what they really want to attain in life.

Chapter 5: Step 4 (Hour 4) - Simplicity Is Best - Simplify Your Life As Much As Possible Without Oversimplifying

Everybody wants to keep things simple as much as possible. Aside from significantly reducing stress levels, this can help you get most of your tasks done in no time. This book section is then dedicated on the important things that you have to simplify in your life.

As discussed in the previous book sections, you have to cut down on your possessions.

These things drain your attention, energy, and bank accounts. These may even keep you away from the people who matter to you the most.

Time commitments can also keep you away from your loved ones if you have so much of these.

As much as possible, release yourself from these commitments. You can assess which of these are worth keeping for a start.

If you have too many goals that you want to reach, you need to cut down on them.

Ideally, one to two main goals at a time is reasonable. By reducing the goals that you aim to accomplish, you can have a better focus on these. Thus, you will have a greater chance of being successful.

Debt is another thing that can always hold you captive if you do not take care of it.

Start reducing it today. If you need help to address this concern, by all means seek that assistance. If you need to sacrifice your luxuries in life to pay off your debts, do so. In the long run, this will help you enjoy freedom in the future.

Chapter 6: Step 5 (Hour 5) - Time Management - Organize Your Time And Live Your Life One Step Ahead Of The Crowd

Time is considered as one of the most important resources that you can ever have because you can never get this back. In this book section are some tips for better time management.

- Create a schedule based a list of all the activities that you need to accomplish within the week.

- Set a specific amount of time for each task that you have to complete within the day.

- Set small chunks of time for interruptions and breaks in between major tasks.

In managing your time, you should keep in mind that you can never get everything done no matter how hard you try. Therefore, you should not take everything too hard on yourself.

Chapter 7: Congratulations! - You're Done Organizing Your Life - What To Do If Clutter Creeps Back In

Clutter recurrence takes place over days, weeks, or days after you performed major organizing moves. Unless you are vigilant, this will be a problem. To help keep your household and workplace from this problem, you have to take note of some important pointers to maintain a clutter-free environment.

- Mostly, it will only take you around five minutes a day to get started with organizing and keeping your surroundings clutter-free. Spend time per day to take out excess items from your storage that you no longer need and arrange the remaining in their respective containers.

- If you have brought something inside your household or workplace, you should make it a point to take out another item to keep the balance

- Before bedtime, make a quick assessment of your household to determine what item to arrange in its proper location.

The main technique to maintain a clutter-free environment is to determine what is really important to you. If you are having a hard time choosing items that should be taken out, you have to prioritize those that can provide you with more space, time, happiness, and money.

Chapter 8: Bonus Tips On Increasing Concentration And Focus!

For your concentration, you can resort to some simple ways on how to boost your concentration. If you are not yet aware of these techniques, it may take some time before you can finally grasp these ideas. Therefore, you just have to be patient about this.

Work on your concentration.

Concentration requires you to take your mind off too many things and focusing on your priorities one at a time.

After laying out your priorities and tasks for the day, you may then decide on what you prefer to focus on at the moment.

This will help you have that need to tune in all of your senses on just one thing. In the long run, this can help you prevent distractions.

As bizarre as it may seem, looking at other people who currently concentrate on their tasks at hand can help you learn more on how to concentrate.

You may somehow imitate their physical cues while doing your tasks. After all, these physical cues can serve as hints on how you can further improve your concentration skills.

Avoiding constant sensory input can also help you focus more on the activities at hand.

Some of the activities that can cause distraction for some people are the following: visual stimulation from television, loud noises, and multitasking. Because these can make concentration a lot difficult, you should minimize or avoid doing these things to prevent inattention to your primary task at hand.

Staying calm can contribute to higher concentration levels.

Deep concentration requires you to direct your energy to what you are doing. More focused energy on the task translates to better concentration in the long run. To help you achieve an ideal state of calmness, you may try out simple exercises like steady breathing even before you start off with your task.

This is also helpful with meditation. Initially, make sure that you will not control your breath in any way. You simply have to observe how you breathe. This will teach you to focus your mind on something per instance. As you continue observing your breath, this will eventually slow down. As your breath slows down, so will your mind. Eventually, you will move into a peaceful and dynamic state of being. However, you will not feel sleepy in the process.

Chapter 9: Bonus Tips On Increasing Motivation And Productivity!

Productivity is considered as a combination of focused efforts and intelligent planning. Staying productive wherever you may go may prove as a challenge for you more than you will ever realize. As each day ends, there is a chance that you may not be completely satisfied with what you accomplished within the day. In this book section, you will learn more on how to improve your productivity by following some helpful tips.

If you can, you have to delegate tasks accordingly or seek help.

This is helpful for both the work and the home setting because you will inevitably encounter large chunks of tasks that you cannot complete within a reasonable amount of time if you decide to do it alone.

To get help from other people, all you have to do is to trust the people you have delegated to help you with work completion. One way to help them take the task more seriously is to present a deadline. You have to make sure that you will provide as much resources as you can for these people so they can come up with the best output that they can.

You should not allow yourself to dwell on unnecessary meetings.

Productivity means maximizing your available time. While it may really be tempting to meet as many people as you can for networking purposes, you also have to focus on your work first.

Knowing the meetings that you have to refuse is also considered important.

If you are the one responsible in setting up the meeting, then you have to focus on important matters that need to be discussed. To make each meeting more productive, you also have to make sure that you will only involve those who are really needed during the meeting process.

Creating to-do lists can help you easily sort out what you have to do for the rest of your day.

If you think you have difficulty sorting your tasks out on paper, acquiring a phone or computer application to assist you with this one can help do wonders for you. If some of your tasks seem larger than the others, they it is a good call to break them down into smaller chunks. Furthermore, you may allot a specific amount of time for each task so you will not end up focusing on a single task longer than you have to. For additional motivation levels, you may even opt to cross out some of the tasks in your list that you have already completed. This will help provide you with a visualization of your progress.

According to experts, taking breaks in between your tasks can help in further improving your productivity rate.

Lipoprotein lipase (LPL) is an enzyme that breaks down adipose tissues in your bloodstream and transforms them into useful energy forms. Experiencing too much stress can highly contribute in lowering LPL. In the long run, this can lead to heart attacks.

One of the most apparent ways to increase productivity is to get rid of most distractions that you may encounter along the way.

This means that you have to disconnect from your social media accounts while doing actual work. If you think that you are really fall behind on the work department, you may consider uninstalling the involved applications from your devices. This will help serve as a reminder that you have larger priorities than browsing these social media sites. In the long run, this will help you do more with less time.

As much as possible, you have to motivate yourself by providing rewards for each significant task completed.

Rewards such as new material possessions or food can help do wonders for you. For some people, getting more sleep is also a good form of reward for a job well done. You may also use the cumulative system to get your rewards.

Chapter 10: Bonus Tips On Eliminating Procrastination For Good!

The procrastination phenomenon is one of the most common problems that people from different age brackets experience on a regular basis. This book section will provide you with some insights on how you can stop procrastination from hampering your success in life.

- Break down your tasks into small components then focus on one aspect at a time.

- Create a timeline for all of your tasks accompanied by their deadlines.

- Regularly interact with people who inspire you to prevent procrastination.

- Have someone whom you can be accountable to.

- Monitor your progress from time to time.

You may formulate your own strategies on how to counteract procrastination so you can make the most out of your life in the long run. Upon learning some ways on how to prevent this, you have to make sure that you will act on your current situation to address the problem as soon as possible.

Conclusion

Thank you again for purchasing the book organizing!

I am extremely excited to pass this information along to you, and I am so happy that you now have read and can hopefully implement these strategies going forward.

I hope this book was able to help you understand the fundamentals of organizing and how to apply these in your household and workplace.

The next step is to get started using this information and to hopefully live a clutter-free life!

Please don't be someone who just reads this information and doesn't apply it, the strategies in this book will only benefit you if you use them!

If you know of anyone else that could benefit from the information presented here please inform them of this book.

Finally, if you enjoyed this book and feel it has added value to your life in any way, please take the time to share your thoughts and post a review on Amazon. It'd be greatly appreciated!

Thank you and good luck!

Preview Of:

Ultimate Manifestation Guide!

<u>Manifestation</u>

The Science Of Manifestation Through Neuroplasticity, Brain Training, NLP Techniques, Creative Visualization, Mindfulness Meditation, And More!

Introduction

I want to thank you and congratulate you for purchasing the book, "Manifestation: Ultimate Manifestation Guide! The Science Of Manifestation Through Neuroplasticity, Brain Training, NLP Techniques, Creative Visualization, Mindfulness Meditation, And More!"

This book contains proven steps and strategies on how to use manifestation techniques to attract the things that you want in life. This book will help you understand the universal law of attraction and help you use it to transform your dreams into reality.

If you feel that your life is getting nowhere and you feel that you cannot control the outcome of your life, this book is for you. This book will help you understand the power of your mind to change your life for the better. This book will also help you realize that you are the master of your life and you have the creative power to map out your destiny.

Thanks again for purchasing this book, I hope you enjoy it!

Chapter 1 : Proof That Manifestation Is Real

The law of attraction is quite popular nowadays. Many celebrities believe it and many claim that they have used it to achieve success and personal transformation. But is it really real?

Well, the law of attraction is a universal law that states that the more you think about something, the more it manifests in your life. So, if you think about success often, if you believe that you are destined for success, you will eventually achieve success. If you think about failure, on the other hand, you will attract people and circumstances that will orchestrate to deliver what you expect – failure.

Have you noticed that whenever you think about a person that you have not thought about for years, he suddenly shows up days later? Have you noticed that if you express interest on, say, traveling to Paris, you will begin to see airline ads and deals that would help you realize your Paris dream vacation? That's huge proof that the law of manifestation is real.

To further illustrate this point, let's take a look at the success stories of celebrities who have deliberately used the law of attraction to bring success into their lives. In the 1980s, Jim Carrey was a struggling actor. He was constantly depressed and he has a hard time trying to make ends meet. He has read about the law of attraction and he decided to give it a try. He wrote himself a check worth ten million dollars and dated the check 1995. He kept the check in his wallet for years. He had nearly forgotten about it. In 1994, Jim Carrey got his breakout roles as Ace Ventura: The Pet Detective and as The Mask. Because of the success of these two films, his market value have significantly increased and he received a ten million dollar check in 1994 for his acting service in the film "Dumb and Dumber".

In 1985, Oprah Winfrey read the book called "The Color Purple". She never stopped thinking about the book and she was literally addicted to it. Years later, her agent called and said that she got an audition for the movie adaptation of "The Color Purple". She wanted the part so bad that she regularly prayed for it. She visualized herself going to the set and shooting the film. She waited for the callback for months and finally, she got the part. Oprah said that the fact that she wanted the part so bad and she believed that she can achieve it and that she is worthy of it is the starting point of her successful career.

The power of thought to influence manifestation was also proven by the water experiment conducted by Dr. Emoto Masaru. Dr. Masaru and his team studies the molecular structure of normal water when frozen. They then asked a monk to bless a glass of water with gratitude and love. They froze the water and they were surprised to see that the molecular structure of the water that was blessed by the monk is different from the unblessed water. The water that was exposed to feelings of love, gratitude, and peace have a beautiful flower-like molecular structure. They then exposed another glass of water to music that is full of angst and hatred. They were also shock to find out that the water exposed to anger have a distorted and ugly molecular form.

The result of this experiment is proof that our thoughts and emotions influence our outer or physical reality. Remember that our body and the world are mainly made of water. Notice that if you wake up in the morning feeling cranky, you will attract negative circumstances because you have emitted negative vibes. If you wake up thinking that it is going to be a bad day, well, it is definitely going to be a bad day. The universe will deliver whatever you expect.

The law of attraction is real and it has helped many people achieve the life that they have always dreamed of. Now is the time for you to use it to your advantage and achieve everything that you have hoped for.

Thanks for Previewing My Exciting Book Entitled:

"Manifestation: Ultimate Manifestation Guide! The Science Of Manifestation Through Neuroplasticity, Brain Training, NLP Techniques, Creative Visualization, Mindfulness Meditation, And More!"

To purchase this book, simply go to the Amazon Kindle store and simply search:

"MANIFESTATION"

Then just scroll down until you see my book. You will know it is mine because you will see my name "Ryan Cooper" underneath the title.

Alternatively, you can visit my author page on Amazon to see this book and other work I have done. Thanks so much, and please don't forget your free bonuses

DON'T LEAVE YET! - CHECK OUT YOUR FREE BONUSES BELOW!

Free Bonus Offer: Get Free Access To The www.LuxyLifeNaturals.com VIP Newsletter!

Once you enter your email address you will immediately get free access to this awesome newsletter!

But wait, right now if you join now for free you will also get free access to the "Anti-Aging Made Easy" free EBook!

To claim both your FREE VIP NEWSLETTER MEMBERSHIP and your FREE BONUS Ebook on ANTI-AGING MADE EASY!

Just Go To:

www.LuxyLifeNaturals.com

www.ingramcontent.com/pod-product-compliance
Lightning Source LLC
Chambersburg PA
CBHW070746180526
45168CB00004B/1545